STOURPORT-ON-SEVERN

Pioneer town of the canal age

Published by English Heritage, Kemble Drive, Swindon SN2 2GZ
www.english-heritage.org.uk
English Heritage is the Government's statutory adviser on all aspects of the historic environment.

Printing 10 9 8 7 6 5 4 3 2 1
Images (except as otherwise shown) © English Heritage, © English Heritage. NMR or
© Crown copyright. NMR.

First published 2007

ISBN 978 1 905624 36 2

Product code 51290

British Waterways, Stourport Forward Market Towns Initiative, Stourport-on-Severn Town Council and
Wyre Forest District Council made financial contributions towards the publication of this book.

British Library Cataloguing in Publication Data
A CIP catalogue record for this book is available from the British Library.

The National Monuments Record is the public archive of English Heritage. For more information,
contact NMR Enquiry and Research Services, National Monuments Record Centre, Kemble Drive,
Swindon SN2 2GZ; telephone (01793) 414600.

Brought to publication by Rachel Howard, Publishing, English Heritage.
Page layout by George Hammond.
Printed in UK by Cambridge Printing.

Front cover
*Stourport's canal basin, with
a backdrop of houses on
York Street. [DP005234]*

STOURPORT-ON-SEVERN

Pioneer town of the canal age

Colum Giles

with contributions by Keith Falconer, Barry Jones and Michael Taylor

Stourport on Severn Civic Society

WYRE FOREST
DISTRICT COUNCIL

ENGLISH HERITAGE

Contents

Acknowledgements

The authors would like to thank a number of individuals and organisations for their help in the production of this book: Simon Roper-Pressdee, Wyre Forest District Council; Pauline Annis, Stourport-on-Severn Civic Society; Elizabeth Turner and Mike Youe, British Waterways; staff at Worcestershire Record Office, Staffordshire Record Office, Gloucestershire Record Office, British Waterways Archive, and Birmingham City Archives. English Heritage staff who have contributed to the project include: Matthew Bentley and Peter Dunn who prepared the graphic illustrations; Mike Hesketh-Roberts who took the photographs; Nick Molyneux who undertook research; Ursula Dugard-Craig and Kate Bould who provided administrative support; and John Cattell who supported the project by making staff resources available. Figures 15, 26, 34, 36 and 37 are from the Anna Carter Collection of Stourport-on-Severn Civic Society and are reproduced with the permission of the Society.

Detail of the clock from the Clock Warehouse, added in 1812. [DP005876]

Foreword

Today many English towns, adjusting to the needs of the 21st century, are turning to the historic environment as a means of reinforcing their identity and distinctiveness, precious attributes in a town's local and regional profile. For Stourport-on-Severn, this special identity is written large in the central part of the town, for there can be few places with such a strong association with a single determining feature – for Stourport, its canal infrastructure – and with a discrete period of development – in this case, the period 1770 to 1850. The regeneration of Stourport depends on many things, but the protection and presentation of its historic environment must lie at the centre of efforts to bring new life to the town. Understanding how Stourport assumed its present form is crucial to public enjoyment of the place and to the planning of change and this book aims to contribute to both aspects by celebrating the town's unique qualities and character. Equally important, this is a work of partnership with national agencies – English Heritage and British Waterways – working with local partners – Wyre Forest District Council, Stourport Forward, Stourport-on-Severn Town Council and Stourport-on-Severn Civic Society – to produce something of benefit to the community. The continuing engagement of all the partners promises well for the future of the town.

Sir Neil Cossons, Chairman English Heritage

Robin Evans, Chief Executive, British Waterways

Stephen Clee, Leader, Wyre Forest District Council

Derek Fradgley, Chief Executive, Stourport Forward

Councillor Michael W Partridge, Town Mayor 2006–07,
Stourport-on-Severn Town Council

Pauline Annis, Chair, Stourport-on-Severn Civic Society

Bunces Close
Bunces Lane
483
482
481
W. A. Roberts
John Acton
484
Bunces Close
Roberts Barn
485
486
487
W. A. Roberts Esqr
Honeysuckle
Sarah Johnson
Bird Lane
Jno Acton
489
488
Barn Close
Follett Esqr
T. Dickens
Wm Hill
T. Hoult
Gilgal
Thos Dickens
Jno Jones
Taylors Hill
Fat Orchard
the Way
Jno Acton
Yard
Jno Barnbrook
Jno Acton
Follett Esqr
Jno Acton
Garden
Fold
Dickens
Hoult
John Palmer
Gardens
Garden
Thos Dickens
Jno Acton
Follett
Jno Acton
Jno Hoult
Gardens
Thos Rea
Gardens
Gardens
Jas Mathews
Orchard
Garden
Pinfold
Follett
Mrs Pats
Orchd
Mr York
Thos Ray
Garden
Follett
River Stour

CHAPTER 1

Lower Mitton before the canal

About 1766, where the river Stour empties itself into the Severn below Mitton, stood a little ale-house called Stourmouth: near this place Brindley has caused a town to be erected, made a port and dock yards, built a new and elegant bridge, established markets, and made it the wonder not only of this county, but of the nation at large.

Dr T R Nash, 1799[1]

In the mid-18th century, inland Britain's industrial development depended on river navigation, the only economic and practical means of moving bulk goods, such as coal and iron, from source to their markets (Fig 1). The River Severn was one of the most important transport routes. It was navigable, for smaller vessels, as far upstream as Pool Quay near Welshpool, and of course opened out into the Bristol Channel, from where coastwise or ocean-going vessels could distribute the products of midland England far and wide. In the higher reaches of the river, Shropshire became an industrial centre of great significance. It had a coalfield, and it was here, in the early decades of the 18th century, that Abraham Darby developed new techniques for producing iron. The great bridge at Ironbridge, built in 1779 using castings from Darby's Coalbrookdale foundries, symbolises the role which this now largely rural area played in a fast-growing industrial economy. Further downstream, Bewdley had already developed as an inland port, where roadways converged at a bridging point to allow the transportation of local produce throughout the Severn network. As it flowed past what was to become Stourport, the river was busy with Severn *trows*, the local form of wooden river-sailing vessels, laden with coal, iron, manufactured goods and agricultural produce.

The Severn was not the only river in the area with importance for the midland industrial economy. Where the Severn was significant mainly as a transport artery, the much smaller River Stour, rising a little to the south-west of Birmingham and discharging into the Severn at what is now Stourport, was utilised as a source of power, first by iron

Figure 1 *A busy scene on the Severn quay at Tewkesbury: stacks of iron await loading, some destined for the forges of the midlands. [Tewkesbury Town Council]*

manufacturers and later by carpet makers around Stourbridge and Kidderminster. In 1789, there were 30 ironworks on the river, drawing on its power to drive slitting mills, forges and wire mills, making it one of the most intensively exploited watercourses in the country. Many of these local industries had been active for decades or even centuries: in the early 18th century Daniel Defoe remarked upon glass and ceramic making at Stourbridge and on Kidderminster woollen cloths.[2]

Lying at the confluence of the Severn and the Stour, to the south of Kidderminster, was the small village of Lower Mitton, the site of the future canal town of Stourport. In contrast to the busy scene of industry along the Stour, and to the future commercial bustle ushered in by the arrival of the canal, the village was, for centuries, a quiet backwater, little more than a means of getting to other places. The road from Worcester entered the village over a bridge crossing the Stour, and then it split, one arm leading north to Kidderminster, the other north-west to Bewdley, the established bridging point over the Severn. Along these roads, a scatter of houses made up the village (Fig 2). There was no centre to the settlement and little sense of cohesion in its plan. The Church of England chapel, the most important communal building, lay detached to the north, well away from roads and houses. The largest resident landowners, the Folliott

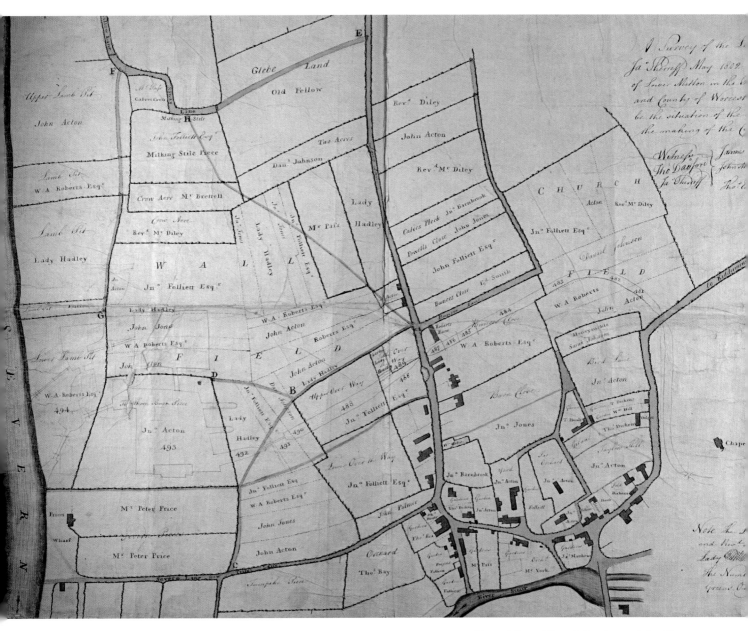

Figure 2 *Lower Mitton before the canal: the village houses are strung out along the principal roads, and the chapel lay on the edge of the settlement to the north. [Reproduced by courtesy of the Staffordshire Record Office D3186/8/1/21]*

3

Figure 3 *Lickhill Manor, an early 18th-century residence, the home of the Folliott family. [DP022209]*

family, lived in relative isolation to the north-west of the village at Lickhill Manor, a splendid early 18th-century house on the banks of the Severn (Fig 3). Most of the village houses were probably little more than cottages for small farmers or agricultural workers. One substantial timber-framed house of 17th-century date survives, but otherwise little remains to indicate the character of the buildings before the late 18th century. Next to the river bridge was a water-powered forge and half a mile to the east of the village was a corn mill, perhaps on the site of the fulling mill recorded in earlier periods, using the power of the Stour for grinding the local farmers' cereals. Leading from the village to the Severn was a track, ending on the river bank at Price's Wharf. From here a ferry took people across the river, and early maps show an old ferry house and a substantial building, probably the Stourmouth Inn (surviving today as the Angel Inn, *see* Fig 53). On the other side of the river was a local curiosity, Redstone Caves, said to have been a hermitage.

CHAPTER 2

The canal arrives

This rustic scene was to change dramatically with the construction of the Staffordshire and Worcestershire Canal and its large basins next to the River Severn and the establishment of a new town at what quickly became a pivotal point of the inland navigation system.

The Staffordshire and Worcestershire Canal (the SWC) was amongst the earliest canals to be built in the period of inland navigation construction in the second half of the 18th century. Its local purpose was to provide the industries of the Black Country with better and cheaper access to sources of supply and to the markets for their products. Canals reduced transport costs hugely, especially for bulky items, and industries flourished once they were able to send their goods by water rather than road. James Perry, the canal's principal promoter, was a Wolverhampton ironfounder and merchant, and he claimed that a new canal would reduce the costs of transporting iron by more than three quarters. Over time the canal had a wider impact, for by connecting with the Trent and Mersey Canal in Staffordshire it formed one arm of the great cross which linked the country's principal ports – London, Bristol, Liverpool and Hull – by inland navigation (Fig 4).

The canal company (SWCC), established at an inaugural meeting in Wolverhampton in January 1766, received parliamentary assent for the canal in May of the same year. Construction began immediately under the supervision of James Brindley, the leading canal engineer of the day. Just a year earlier, Brindley had completed the pioneering Bridgewater Canal linking the Duke of Bridgewater's coal mines at Worsley with Manchester, a distance of 14 miles (23 kilometres). The SWC was a more ambitious venture altogether. The chosen route between the Trent and Mersey Canal at Great Haywood and the Severn at Stourmouth was much longer (46 miles/73 kilometres) and involved the construction of 43 locks.

Brindley was to act very much as consulting engineer. The construction of the canal was the responsibility of a local team appointed by the canal company and led by John Baker, a gentleman of Wolverhampton, as Clerk of Works. Baker was ably assisted by an Under Clerk, John Green, who probably undertook most of the practical side of the work. Much of the earth moving was done by contract, but the construction of the locks and bridges was achieved by direct labour, which, in these pioneer days, had to learn on the job. Thus Thomas Dadford, who was originally appointed in 1767 as a carpenter, was responsible for all the locks and the basins, while his assistant, Mr Pyatt, worked mostly on bridges. On the other hand, some of the contractors, such as John Beswick, were much more experienced, having worked on navigation schemes around the country for more than a decade.

Despite this division of labour, building work appears to have encountered few problems, and on 1 April 1771 the *Birmingham Gazette* was able to report that the southern half of the canal was 'open for business with Wharfs and Warehouses made and Wharfingers fixed'. In this announcement the new terminus by the Severn, which Brindley had hitherto referred to as Newport, was for the first time called Stourport.

Building the canal basins: the first phase

The new southern terminus on the Severn was more than simply a junction of navigation routes. It was, primarily, an installation which allowed the trans-shipment of goods between different types of water craft – Severn trows, best suited for river navigation, and narrowboats, designed for canal navigation. The main requirement at the trans-shipment point was, therefore, a large area – an inland dock or basin – which all types of craft could use to offload to the adjacent wharves or take on cargoes for their onward journey.

Suitable land for the necessary installations was purchased in 1768 near the confluence of the rivers Severn and Stour. Here, away from the village of Lower Mitton and a little upstream from the old ferry crossing, there lay an expanse of level ground, clear of the flood plain but well situated in relation to the best route for the canal as it followed the course of the River Stour. The SWCC at first bought two fields, amounting to seven acres, to accommodate its basin. For the canal itself, the company

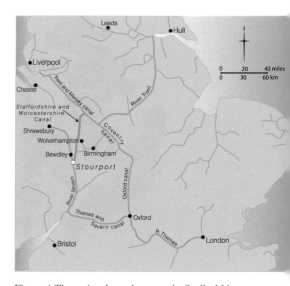

Figure 4 *The national canal system: the Staffordshire and Worcestershire Canal provided a link between the River Severn and the midland canal network.*

only purchased a narrow strip of land sufficient for its line. In September 1769 it acquired 'a close of land near the River Severn in which bricks are now making',[3] thus providing itself with control over the supply of the huge number of bricks which the canal required. It also purchased a plot of land alongside the River Stour to erect a water-powered 'engine' to supply the basin via a feeder and aqueduct. The construction of the basin and all the adjacent buildings was probably the principal engineering project in the whole length of the canal, and it must have required a considerable workforce, to be based for an extended period in Lower Mitton. The workforce was perhaps partly recruited from the local agricultural population, but where it was housed is not clear. Certainly the SWCC provided little in the way of permanent housing on its own estate.

The construction of the first canal basin (the Upper Old Basin), two acres in extent, and its associated buildings represented a major investment for the SWCC. It was one of the great achievements of the Canal Age, if not in scale then at least in the pioneering vision of how to provide the most up-to-date facilities for a transport interchange (Fig 5). The nature of the basin closely reflected the type of traffic which was anticipated. The principal bulk cargoes were Staffordshire coal, on the way to markets down the Severn and beyond, timber from the Wyre Forest, and iron from the Forest of Dean destined for the forges of the midlands ironworking area. Manufactured products also passed through the basin in transit to distant markets: iron goods from the Black Country, pottery and glass from Staffordshire, and Lancashire textiles were all trans-shipped in Stourport. Agricultural produce tended to flow mainly the other way, locally grown food and hops satisfying the demand from the growing industrial towns of the Black Country. An idea of the operation and the cargoes handled by the basins is given in leases of the 'Old Iron Warehouse' granted in 1799 for 21 years to carriers such as Jonathan Worthington, Peter Samuel, William Owen, and Wall & Banks. These specified in great detail the rates fixed for the 'stowage, weighing and cranage' of a huge variety of goods ranging from building materials, nails and iron pots by the ton to crates of glass and earthenware, cotton and wool bales, hogsheads of liquor and various perishable commodities.[4]

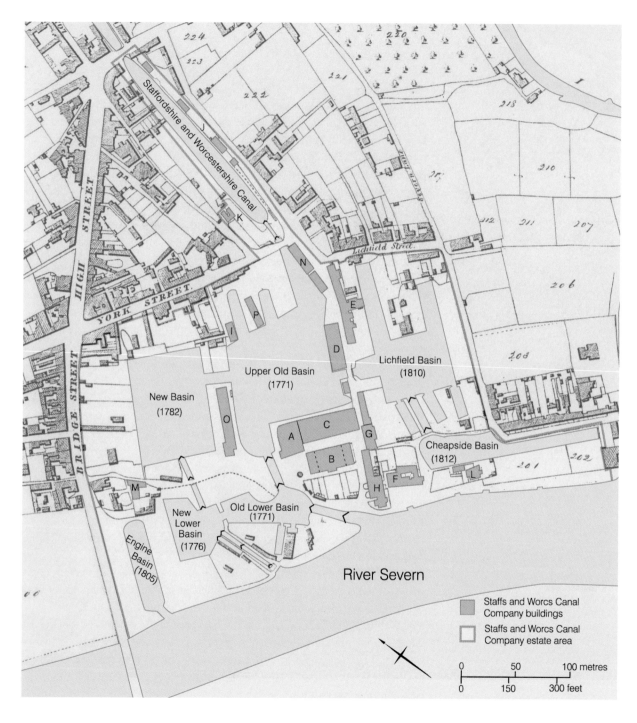

Staffordshire and Worcestershire Canal

HIGH STREET

YORK STREET

BRIDGE STREET

K

N

P

I

E

D

O

A

C

B

G

H

F

L

M

New Basin
(1782)

Upper Old Basin
(1771)

Lichfield Basin
(1810)

Cheapside Basin
(1812)

New
Lower
Basin
(1776)

Old Lower Basin
(1771)

Engine
Basin
(1805)

River Severn

Lichfield Street.

224
223
222
221
220
218
210
211
207
212
206
205
201
202

Staffs and Worcs Canal
Company buildings

Staffs and Worcs Canal
Company estate area

0   50   100 metres
0   150   300 feet

Figure 5 *The canal infrastructure in Stourport: this plan shows the basins at their full extent in the early 19th century. [Based on Lower Mitton Tithe Map, 1849, Worcs RO, BA1572 5760/428]*

Key

A   *Iron Warehouse (1771); later offices and lock-keeper's house*

B   *Tontine Hotel (Stourport Inn) and Corner Houses (1773)*

C   *Shed Warehouse (c1772)*

D   *Long Room Warehouse (c1772)*

E   *Mart Lane house, warehouses and office (18th century)*

F   *Angel Inn (18th century)*

G   *Ames and Worthington's Warehouses (18th century)*

H   *Stabling for Stourport Inn and lock-keeper's house*

I   *North Warehouse (18th century)*

J   *Timber wharfs (18th century)*

K   *Wharfinger's House (18th century)*

L   *Four small tenements (18th century)*

M   *Engine house (Boulton and Watt 1805)*

N   *Joynson's Warehouse (early 19th century)*

O   *Clock Warehouse (early 19th century)*

P   *York Street Warehouse (19th century)*

Some of these goods – especially coal – could be stacked in the open air, and the generous wharves around the first basin offered extensive storage space. More valuable or vulnerable cargoes, however, required secure shelter, and from the earliest years the SWCC provided warehousing. On the east side of the basin stood what was called the Long Room (Fig 6), a two-storey warehouse directly alongside the water, with two waterside loading hoists to lift goods to the upper floor. One of the earliest canal warehouses in the country, it was demolished in the 1950s. Set back a little from the south side of the basin were two

Figure 6 *The Long Room (shown here on the left), now demolished, lay on the east side of the original basin. [AA49/4245]*

Figure 7 *(left) The Iron Warehouse, one of the earliest of the canal warehouses and conspicuous because of its rounded corner. [DP005232]*

Figure 8 *(right) The canal basin and the Iron and Shed Warehouses, depicted in early 19th-century views. [Reproduced by courtesy of the Staffordshire Record Office D3186/8/1/30; DP022160, DP022161]*

warehouses, a long single-storey shed (soon raised to two storeys) and beside it the Iron Warehouse, with its distinctive rounded corner (Fig 7). Only the Iron Warehouse survives. Built by 1771, when the SWC Committee ordered that 'a compting house be made with all speed adjoining the Iron Warehouse',[5] it is possibly the earliest surviving canal warehouse in the country. The adjoining British Waterways' offices were built in the early 19th century and incorporated a lock-keeper's house. The two warehouses are depicted in a pair of early drawings, showing barges in the basin, cranes on the wharf, and cargoes stacked in tidy piles waiting for dispatch (Fig 8).

The dominating presence in the early years of the canal basin, and still today, was the great Tontine Hotel (Fig 9), at first called the Areley Inn, later the Stourport Inn. It is thought that the building took its present name from the title of a society which used the premises. The building was constructed to provide a hotel in the centre and four houses in the end wings. To warrant this large investment, the SWCC must have seen both the need for such a building and its potential for profit. The town of Stourport was little more than a plan in the first years of the canal's operating life and lacked facilities for accommodation and entertainment, and the four dwellings contained originally within the Tontine were at least a gesture towards the provision of housing for company servants or patrons. Next to the Inn was a range of stabling for the horses of either the users of the inn or the SWCC itself.

Figure 9 *(right) The Tontine Hotel as it appears now. [DP022093]*

In the 1770s, **THE TONTINE HOTEL** formed the centrepiece in the new enterprise of Stourport. The Tontine dominated the scene, its substantial façade addressing the Severn waterfront, its back turned to the canal basins and the fields that were yet to become the new town. Built by the SWCC to promote and facilitate development of the port, the hotel was probably completed in 1773, perhaps being the 'Capital House' referred to in the minutes of the Canal Proprietors.[i] Designed by an unnamed hand, although perhaps attributable to Thomas Dadford, the SWCC engineer, the building has little architectural pretension: its simple brick façade, stretched to seven bays, lacks the elegance normally associated with Georgian design. Nevertheless, the Tontine is an exceptional building, the earliest canal company hotel in England, with no known antecedents. It set a precedent for future transport hotels, including the renowned railway company hotels of the 19th century.

The hotel provided accommodation for canal and river travellers and for the wealthy visitors who, from the first years, congregated in Stourport and held regattas on the canal basins. It was also the meeting place for the canal company shareholders and committee, and it gave accommodation for merchants engaged in business at the port. The hotel occupied the five central bays of the building and extended back into the central rear wing.

The main vestibule opened onto a grand staircase leading up to a first-floor ballroom, as well as at least nine bedrooms on the upper floors. In 1882, J Randell, writing in *The Severn Valley*, claimed that in its heyday the hotel had 'rooms sufficient to make up a hundred beds',[ii] a statement suggesting that rooms were intended for multiple occupancy.

The building was always more than a hotel. Its distinctive E-shaped plan appears to have been intended to permit the provision of integral houses, referred to as 'four corner houses' on Thomas Smith's 1810 plan of Stourport. These were contained in the end wings of the building: the 1776 view of the basin shows doorways leading into the front houses, while the houses at the rear were entered from the back wall. The houses were arranged in pairs, planned as a mirror image in each wing and based on a two-room unit, with services in small outbuildings between the wings. In each house, the entrance led directly into a large kitchen, with a substantial open fireplace. A respectable parlour was located beyond, adjacent to a good staircase, which provided access to rooms on the upper floors, as well as to cellars. These houses, being considerably more substantial than workers' cottages, were probably intended for merchants, although it is likely that occupiers let some rooms as lodgings.

As the nature of canal business altered, changes were made to the Tontine, including the subdivision of the houses, probably shortly after the 1810 survey. New doorways were formed on the side elevations and cramped staircases inserted in the original kitchens. In the mid-19th century, the ends of the hotel were

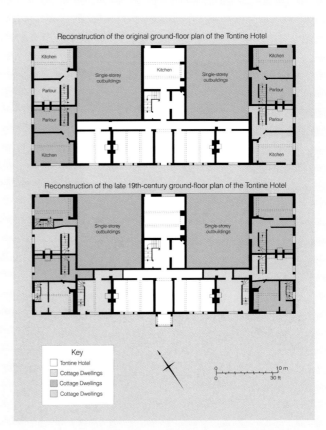

Reconstruction of the original ground-floor plan of the Tontine Hotel

Reconstruction of the late 19th-century ground-floor plan of the Tontine Hotel

Key
Tontine Hotel
Cottage Dwellings
Cottage Dwellings
Cottage Dwellings

divided-off, creating two more cottages, giving a total of at least nine separate dwellings. The Tontine underwent extensive internal alterations, during the 1970s, although the grand staircase and basement services survive. The cottages were left largely untouched and retain much of their early character, including fireplaces carrying the canal company mark.

i Staffs RO, Minute Book of proprietors of SWC, 17 March 1772
ii Randell 1882

A SOUTH WEST PROSPECT or PERSPECTIVE VIEW of STOUR PORT

To the PROPRIETORS of the Staffordshire and Worcestershire CANAL This PLATE is humbly inscrib'd
by their most obedient Servant James Sherriff

Figure 10 *Sherriff's view of the canal basin, 1776.*
[The Waterways Archive Gloucester]

The pioneering achievement of the SWCC in its first years is
strikingly depicted in a print of 1776 (Fig 10), which gives some of the
'frontier' feel to the venture. The canal basin and its associated buildings
appear as new and alien intrusions into a rural landscape. The scene is
one of trade and activity: trows ply on the river in the foreground, there
are barges and trows in the basin and boats being built near to the river,
piles of goods are heaped on the wharves, and large buildings –
warehouses by the basin, the Tontine Hotel on the terrace above the river,
and stabling and lower lock-keeper's dwelling on the slope leading down
to the river bank – dominate the picture. Of a town there is no sign, but it
was doubtless developing out of view, linked to the right bank of the
Severn by the new bridge, built by the SWCC and opened in 1775,
shown in the foreground.

CHAPTER 3

The later development of the canal estate

For 20 years, the Staffordshire and Worcestershire Canal (SWC) was the only waterway connecting the midlands with the River Severn, and it prospered under this monopoly. The volume of traffic passing through Stourport grew rapidly, and the first installations soon proved inadequate. By 1782 a large New Basin, to the west of the first, was in operation, linked both to the earlier basin and, by a second set of locks and another intermediate basin, to the river (*see* Fig 5). Graving docks, for boat building and repair, were also constructed next to the river, and two small dry docks, with adjacent small warehouses, were cut into the wharves on the northern side of the Old Basin: one of these warehouses survived until 1996 (Fig 12). Further extension of the dock area was warranted in the early 19th century. In 1806–10 the SWCC built the Inner or Lichfield Basin, connected to the Upper Old Basin by a channel bridged by Mart Lane and with two dry docks on the north side. It was soon extended by a lock to a lower basin in the area known as Cheapside and a plan of 1810 by Thomas Smith indicates that this latter basin was part of the original concept (Fig 13). There was probably an intention of locking

Figure 11 *(left) The Clock Warehouse, built in the early 19th century when the basins were extended.* [DP005230]

Figure 12 *(right) One of the small warehouses added to the Upper Old Basin.* [© Timothy W L Cooper, OP/04381]

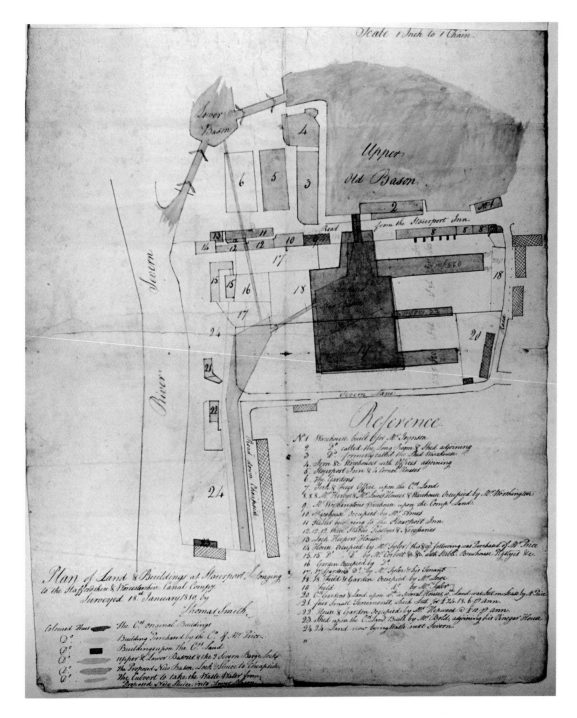

Figure 13 *Smith's plan of the basins, 1810. The key gives the uses of the main buildings:*

1 *Warehouse;*

2 *Long Room and Shed;*

3 *Shed Warehouse;*

4 *Iron Warehouse and offices;*

5 *Stourport Inn;*

7 *Office (York and Frees);*

8 *Two houses and warehouse;*

9 *Warehouse;*

10 *Warehouse;*

11 *Inn stables;*

12 *Stables, pigsties, etc;*

13 *Lock-keeper's house;*

15 *House, stables, brewhouse, etc*

[Reproduced by courtesy of the Staffordshire Record Office D3186/8/1/30/116; DP022157]

down into the river from the Cheapside Basin but this never transpired and it remained a cul-de-sac until it was infilled and its site developed for the town's gasworks in 1865.

The company also erected a further three warehouses around the Upper Old Basin, two along the eastern side and the third on the wharf between it and the New Basin. This latter warehouse was surmounted by an ornate clock in 1812, largely paid for by public subscription (*see* Fig 11). A limited amount of housing was also built on the canal estate, on the east side of Mart Lane, where there is a short terrace of three-storeyed brick houses (Fig 14), attached at the south end to a lower warehouse, occupied in 1810 by one of the principal canal carriers.

Figure 14 *In the late 18th century the canal company built a short row of buildings on Mart Lane: in 1810 it provided two houses and accommodation for two of the principal canal carriers: Jonathan Worthington occupied the low warehouse, and York and Frees used the end house as offices. [DP005184]*

Figure 15 *The canalside maintenance yard.*
[Stourport-on-Severn Civic Society; DP022135]

North of the Upper Old Basin, the SWCC acquired narrow strips of land on either side of the canal. In 1802 the eastern side was used as a timber wharf and timber yard, with a weighing machine and shop. The western side was developed somewhat later as a maintenance yard and linked to the timber wharves by a wooden footbridge (Fig 15).

Water Supply

The SWC is a summit canal – it rises through 12 locks from Great Haywood in the valley of the Trent, crosses the watershed at Gailey, and then falls from Compton through 31 locks to Stourport on the Severn. Along its length, the canal was supplied by water from nearby rivers and streams, supplemented by reservoirs and pumping engines. There were eventually eight reservoirs in all. The basins at Stourport, with their large barge locks into the Severn, required even more water than came down the canal. Initially the canal company overcame this by abstracting water from the River Stour via a weir below Mitton Bridge and raising it by a waterwheel-driven pump into a feeder aqueduct, whence it was conveyed by a covered feeder into the north-east corner of the Upper Old Basin (Fig 16).

Figure 16 *This detail from Sherriff's map of 1802 shows the original water-supply system, with water taken from the Stour to a pump house (shown here to the bottom centre of figure) and pumped up to the Upper Old Basin.*
[The Waterways Archive Gloucester]

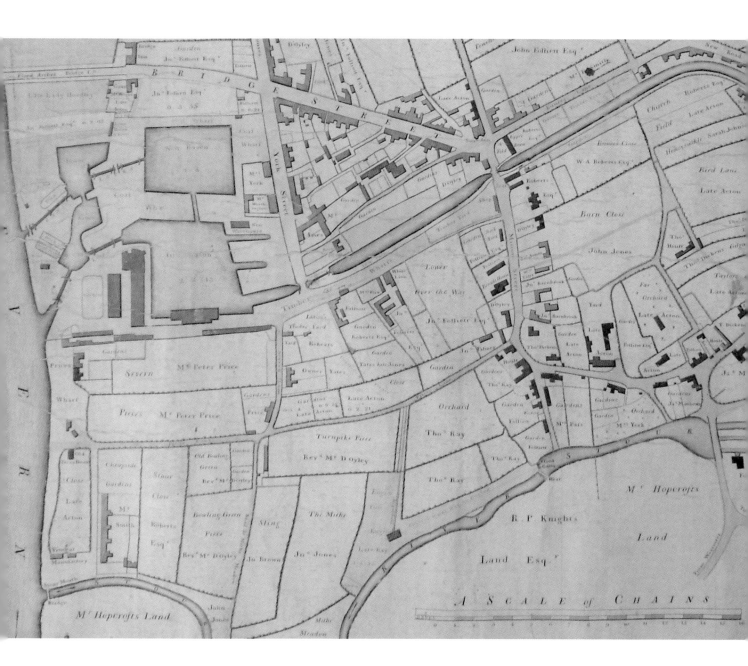

The addition of new basins soon made the original water supply inadequate, and in 1804 it was determined to replace it by a steam-powered system. A pumping engine was ordered from Boulton and Watt, the premier steam engine builders of the time, and the beam engine and pumping machinery were manufactured at the company's new foundry at Smethwick. A fine set of drawings survives to show the location and arrangement of the pumping installation (Fig 17), which took water from a new 'Engine Arm' inlet on the Severn just below Stourport Bridge. The engine house was erected next to some limekilns and water was raised in a metal standpipe some 32 feet (9.7 metres) to a launder feeding the New Basin. The installation must have proved fully adequate, as in 1808 the SWCC leased the original waterwheel engine site on the River Stour to a consortium 'for the purpose of converting the Engine House into a Wire Mill'.[6] The Boulton and Watt beam engine was reputedly scrapped during the First World War, but the engine house survives in an altered form (Fig 18).

The canal estate: decline

The SWCC enjoyed four decades of expansion and prosperity. The basins at Stourport were regarded as something of a phenomenon, attracting visitors eager to witness the evidence of economic and technological progress. In 1813 a commentator noted that 'the quays are covered with warehouses for the reception of goods with large stacks of coal, piles of timber, iron, alabaster etc, etc. It is in every respect a river port, or emporium of inland navigation'.[7] An idea of all this activity can be gained from a reconstruction of the scene as it might have been at the time (Fig 19).

The period of prosperity for the canal was, however, relatively short lived. The annual dividends, which had increased threefold between 1785 and 1806, had peaked by 1815. The opening of the Worcester and Birmingham Canal in 1816 gave Birmingham a shorter route to the south-west avoiding the vagaries of the River Severn above Worcester,

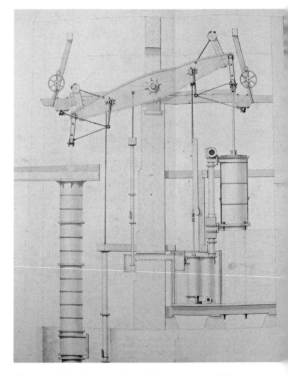

Figure 17 *The 1804 drawing of the Boulton and Watt steam pumping engine. [Birmingham City Archives MS 3147/5/595 Staffordshire and Worcestershire Canal Engine, 1804; AA049732]*

Figure 18 *The 1804 engine house today, recognisable by the distinctive shape needed to accommodate a pumping engine. [DP022094]*

where vessels could be delayed for weeks in the summer when the water was low; only after 1846 were locks built on the Severn to improve navigation. The rise of new industries in the town itself and the continuing productivity of the ironworks and collieries in its hinterland buffered the canal company against immediate recession, but after 1816 there was little further investment in the town's canal facilities. Thereafter the company concentrated its efforts on attempts to improve the River Severn itself. A map of the canal estate, totalling 17 acres (6.9 hectares), was produced in 1849, but it is a telling indication of stagnation that it shows little change since the early 19th century. The conclusion is that after 1815 there had been a fairly complete halt to investment in new canal facilities. There was to be no recovery, for the development of a

Figure 19 *Stourport in the early 19th century: the canal basins are the scene of busy commercial activity, and Lichfield and Cheapside Basins are under construction. In the background the town, partly built up along its main streets, soon gives way to fields.*

national railway system ensured that Stourport's canal facilities became increasingly outmoded. The SWCC continued in being, mainly as a carrier of coal, until finally taken under the wing of the British Transport Commission on 1 January 1948. Its assets were transferred to the British Waterways Board following the passing of the 1962 Transport Act.

Stourport – the premier Canal Town

Stourport was not the only town to owe its existence to a canal. At the beginning of the 19th century there were at least three other canal towns of note – Runcorn, Ellesmere Port and Goole. These four towns initially shared some common characteristics but Stourport was the pioneer and is arguably the finest. In 1800, when its population was over 1600, it was also the largest and most fully developed canal town. Runcorn, the brainchild of the Duke of Bridgewater, is almost exactly contemporary with Stourport, with a warehouse, some workers' housing and other buildings including the Duke's own Bridgewater House provided by 1775. But, built on a steep slope with a flight of ten locks down to the Mersey, it was very much a settlement of two parts and lacks the canal identity of Stourport. The Stourport basins had the Tontine Hotel dating from 1773, quite overshadowing in scale Bridgewater House at Runcorn and rivalled only by the Banks Arms in Goole built almost fifty years later.

 Both Stourport and Runcorn initially became 'places of resort'. But while Runcorn (and Ellesmere Port somewhat later) rather improbably became salt-water bathing resorts and were to continue so until the mid-19th century, Stourport attracted 'People of Fashion in their Carriages' and 'Regattas were not unusual'.[8] This trade, however, was shorter lived. All four towns expanded greatly throughout the canal era but this is where the similarities end. The other three towns, being situated with access to estuaries, developed coastal and international trade and burgeoned in the later 19th century, whereas Stourport's water-borne trade, dependent on the Severn (barely navigable by larger vessels), withered in the face of railway competition. However, the town's recession was to be its architectural saviour – whereas the other canal towns have become unrecognisable as such, Stourport has retained its unique identity.

CHAPTER 4

The development of the town

The Staffordshire and Worcestershire Canal Company had a limited and fixed objective: it existed to run a canal. Unlike other canal companies, such as the Aire and Calder Company (builders of Goole, in Yorkshire) and the Ellesmere and Chester Canal Company (belatedly, at Ellesmere Port), and unlike some railway companies of a later age, it chose not to divert its attention to the establishment of a new town. Its land purchases were sufficient only for the canal itself and for the first stages of the canal basin. It did, however, exercise a very strong economic hold over the town in its early decades. It prompted urban development through the construction of key facilities like the bridge over the River Severn and the Tontine Hotel, provided a slaughterhouse, and helped to finance a new market hall, schools, and a police force. Nevertheless, Stourport is not a company town, rather one which developed opportunistically through speculative investment. Early on it became clear that the canal basin was going to generate considerable business, that services would be required to facilitate normal life and trade, and that opportunities existed for profitable investment in bricks and mortar.

The task of transforming an agricultural parish into a commercial centre was a highly complex one. The pre-existing landholding pattern was fragmented, with a number of different people owning land, in the form of fields, on the site of the future town. Within a few years a new pattern had been imposed on the landscape, one which cut across the existing field divisions and created a multitude of new property boundaries. What rights the former landholders retained in the new properties, and what role they had in the setting out of the town, are not clear, but some sort of general agreement among them about the desirability of promoting development, together with some surrendering of rights, must be assumed. Some of the properties developed in the first stages of the town's construction appear to have been let on 200-year leases.

The key to the formation of the town was the establishment of a street pattern, as this provided the framework for the laying out of individual plots. The existing roads provided some of this framework, but the decisive shaping force was the driving of a new road – Bridge Street in its lower part, High Street above – which became the spine of the new town. It ran south-west from the junction of the Worcester–Bewdley route with

Georgian Stourport: the first streets were lined with houses built in good brick and showing a variety of window styles. [DP022128]

the canal, to cross the Severn by means of a new bridge. This new bridge, of three stone arches, was opened in 1775 (*see* Fig 36), much to the consternation of the people of Bewdley, previously the main river crossing point. A second axis was developed, in the form of York Street and New Street, on a north-west–south-east line. York Street provided part of the circuit of roads around the canal basin and provided valuable properties with direct access to wharfs. However, New Street was a dead end, with a name which suggested that it was an afterthought, laid out to cater for continuing demand for residential development. Beyond this core, other streets were gradually developed – Lombard Street and Foundry Street to the north; Lion Hill, Lichfield Street and Severn Lane to the east; and Lickhill Lane (the old turnpike route to Bewdley, now Lickhill Road) to the west (*see* inside back cover).

The Canal basin opened for business in 1771 and the Tontine Hotel was in use in 1773. The town developed around this nucleus. Leases on newly-defined properties in High Street were let from at least as early as 1777, houses in New Street may have been built after 1784, and in 1803 Thomas Wright, a timber merchant of Stourport, agreed to 'lay out and expend in good and proper building materials with bricks, stone and mortar timbers, timber stuff boards tiles and slates at least the sum of £500' on properties in or behind Bridge Street.[9] Therefore, the decades after the opening of the canal were, if not ones of incessant and frenetic building activity, at least ones of solid progress in the construction of a new town, albeit a new town with only four main streets. Progress can be

Figure 20 *The principal streets of Stourport are lined with houses of pleasing Georgian design: (far left) High Street [DP005879] (left) New Street [DP022115] (right) Lichfield Street [DP005220]*

measured in the descriptions provided by John Wesley on his repeated preaching visits: in 1787, he found Stourport 'a small, new-built village'; a year later he noted the existence of two or three streets; and in 1790 he thought that the town was 'twice as large as two years ago'.[10] By 1801 the population of Lower Mitton (including the town of Stourport) was 1603, and ten years later, it had reached 2352. The rate of growth slackened thereafter as the economic fortunes of the town began to falter, but this should not obscure the fact that, remarkably, a substantial town had sprung into being in the course of a few decades. Stourport belongs to a small group of entirely new towns – industrial, port, spa and resort – built in England in the 18th century as economic growth began to radically change the face of the country.

The character of the new town

Stourport could have become a shanty town, a chaos of cheap, unregulated building devoid of design quality and constructed in poor materials. But this did not happen. Instead, an urban settlement of modest distinction arose around the canal basin, with strong building lines along the main street frontages and with houses and other structures built of good materials to restrained, simple and pleasing Georgian designs (Fig 20). How this happened is not entirely clear. The tone may

have been set by the canal company through its provision of solid, substantial buildings such as the Tontine and the housing on Mart Lane, but the actual achievement was the result of the efforts of numerous individuals, perhaps working consciously or otherwise to a set of common assumptions and aspirations about what the new town should be.

Stourport is built of brick, chosen because it was available locally and because it was cheap and of good quality. The canal company made its own bricks from the first years, and in 1811 a field next to the Severn was noted as 'having a most valuable Clay Mine under the same … The clay in the adjoining piece has lately been advantageously worked out'.[11] The bricks produced in these small brickyards were used throughout the town: Flemish-bond brickwork is commonly used on the façades of the better buildings, and shaped, moulded bricks were used in bracketed eaves cornices to give a decorative finish to street frontage walls; plainer buildings have simple dentilled cornices (Fig 21). Tiles were used for the roofing material originally, and some buildings retain these locally made products, but improvements in transport, partly, of course, brought about by the canal, allowed the introduction of Welsh slate during the 19th century.

Figure 21 *The brickwork of the houses in the main street is of good quality, and decorative cornices, with either moulded brackets or simple dentils, finish the walls at the eaves (middle and right). [DP022076, DP022079, DP022056]*

The impression of unity provided by the use of common building materials is strengthened in the principal streets by the adoption of the three-storeyed terrace form. What we see today, however, is the result of decades of evolution, beginning in the 1770s and continuing well into the 19th century: High Street, for example, retained gaps in its frontage as late as the mid-19th century. Our view, therefore, of a completed town scene could not have been shared by contemporaries. Despite this, the rapid development of the early decades at least pointed the way to the destination and provided a vocabulary of form and style. However, Stourport's terraces are not single-phase developments built in a single campaign by a developer, like those commonly found in London, Bath or contemporary Liverpool. Instead, they are made up of many individual units, with straight or ragged joints in the brickwork revealing the divisions between building phases (Fig 22). The fabric of the town, therefore, reflects the absence of a single controlling proprietor and

Figure 22 *The terraces in the main streets were built in stages – a straight joint in High Street (left) and a toothed corner, High Street, anticipating the keying-in of brickwork and avoiding a straight joint (right). [DP022126, DP022077]*

reveals the activities of a host of small-scale investors, in some streets over a prolonged period, building either for their own use or to derive an income from their property. For example, on the north side of New Street it seems that there was a gradual south-east to north-west progression of building phases, with each new house depending on the end wall of its neighbour to the south-east. One early name for the street – Club Houses (shown on a map of 1802) – suggests that the housing may have been built in sequence by a terminating building club.

The superficial uniformity provided by the terrace form is broken up through variations in architectural detail which give diversity and character. In the four main streets, many of the original doorcases have been replaced by shop fronts, but where they survive they display a range of Classical features and elegant glazing to fanlights (Fig 23). While windows in the same streets are mainly of hung-sash form, with frames flush to the wall, lintels show variety in their decorative treatment: some have plain rubbed-brick wedge lintels, but many others have raised

Figure 23 *Doorcases in the main streets of Stourport.*
[DP005840, DP005185, DP005216, DP022081]

stone or stucco lintels, incised in a number of ways (Fig 24). In the appearance of houses, the objective for the builder clearly was to conform to a general pattern, but to express individuality through detail.

In two areas of the new town, the three-storeyed terrace was not employed. The south side of York Street was never fully developed for residential purposes: much of the land here, running down to the basins, was owned by the canal company and used by carriers as open wharfage, where goods could be stored while awaiting onward journeys by narrowboat or trow. The rest of the land was built up in three main blocks, a short terrace at the west end, continuing round from Bridge Street, and, in the central part of the street, two of the grandest dwellings in town, each one detached in its own grounds, although still standing

Figure 24 *In the houses in the main streets, window lintels have a variety of designs. [DP005202, DP022124, DP005862]*

directly next to the street. They were built by two of the wealthiest canal carriers of the town: York House (Fig 25) was built by Aaron York, who in 1776 obtained permission from SWCC to carry bricks for housebuilding over company land and its neighbour was occupied in 1802 by John Worthington. The two houses, both enjoying direct access from their cellars to gardens and thence to the canal wharf, symbolise very clearly where the real money was to be made in the new town.

The other part of the central area which was not lined with housing was the south-east side of Bridge Street. The north-west side of the street has a number of fine late 18th-century houses and presents a fully-developed frontage, albeit of a mix of two- and three-storeyed houses.

Figure 25 *York House, York Street, built and occupied by one of the principal canal carriers and with direct access to the Upper Old Basin.* [DP022114]

Figure 26 *Bridge Street in the early 20th century, fully built up with housing on one side, but with commercial buildings backing on to wharves on the other. [Stourport-on-Severn Civic Society; DP022136]*

Over much of the length of the south-east side of the street, however, there are no early buildings, and contemporary maps reveal that development here was partial. The reason for this is that this area provided immensely important access to the canal basin, and any building here would have obstructed road traffic moving to and from the wharfs. A strongly commercial character therefore dominated this part of Bridge Street, and it is likely that coal, timber and many other bulk commodities began or ended their land journey here (Fig 26). The disuse of the canal basin for commercial purposes allowed the development of this side of Bridge Street in the 20th century, and the present shops probably replace warehousing and open wharfage.

The sort of housing provided in the new town was varied. At the top of the scale were houses like York House, the homes of the wealthiest

commercial families living in some style, with elegant rooms to front and rear (Fig 27). Most of the houses in the central part of the town are smaller: some are of three bays, others of two or even just a single bay, but even the smallest of these attempts to fit into the prevailing polite architectural style. Many houses are not as large as they appear from the outside: an impressive three-storeyed frontage to the street on High Street, for example, might disguise a house that is just a single room deep. Away from the centre, plainer and simpler brick houses are found. For example, in Lombard Street, just a few steps from High Street, the change is immediately apparent, for here the houses, although of three storeys, have simple segmental-arched windows and a plain sill band over the façade (Fig 28). Furthermore, arched openings give access by a narrow passage to courts, once occupied by small houses at the rear of plots (Fig 29). The cottages in Foundry Street have wide, segmental-headed windows instead of vertical sashes (Fig 30), and many of the cottages in Gilgal, perhaps late 18th- or early 19th-century rebuilding of earlier houses, are more informally grouped and much

Figure 27 *The stair landing and plaster detail in York House, perhaps the grandest house in Stourport. [DP022046, DP022045]*

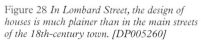

Figure 28 *In Lombard Street, the design of houses is much plainer than in the main streets of the 18th-century town.* [DP005260]

Figure 29 *A narrow entrance to a court, numbered by a sign over the archway.* [DP022061]

Figure 30 (left, top)
In Foundry Street the houses have vernacular features, including segmental-headed windows, and lack the decorative qualities of houses in the main streets. [DP005259]

Figure 31 (left, bottom)
Houses in Gilgal: these follow the line of the old roads through Lower Mitton. [DP022064]

Figure 32 (below)
No.19 Gilgal, with its extravagant display of fenestration, must have been very conspicuous to travellers. [DP022065]

Figure 33 *In Mitton Street, houses set back from the road in large gardens preserve the layout and rural character of the former village of Lower Mitton. [DP005845]*

simpler in style (Fig 31). Even here, however, in the former village of Lower Mitton, elegant and fine houses can be found. The extraordinary fenestration of 19 Gilgal (Fig 32) must have been intended as an eye-catcher for road travellers, and while other houses of early 19th-century date might not have had the prestige location of Lichfield Street or New Street they enjoyed more space, being set back in gardens and retaining the village feel of an earlier era (Fig 33).

The town acquires facilities

A town needs more than houses and commercial open space, and very quickly there developed in and around the core of the settlement a range of important facilities which made Stourport a place of some significance, rivalling Bewdley in the trappings of urban life which it could offer. The growing importance of Lower Mitton was acknowledged in 1790, when the Church of England chapel was rebuilt in larger form to provide better accommodation for worship (Fig 34) and, perhaps, to attempt to ward off

Figure 34 *The 1790 church, photographed before demolition in the 1880s. [Stourport-on-Severn Civic Society; DP022133]*

the incursions of the Methodists. Many of the leading entrepreneurs – among them the Baldwin family and Aaron York – were Methodists, and John Wesley made three visits to Stourport in the early years of its existence. Already by the 1780s, there were two nonconformist chapels in the heart of the new town. Hidden behind High Street, down Parkes Passage, is the Wesleyan Methodist Chapel with its adjacent manse and school house. A plain cement-rendered brick box externally, the chapel has a wonderful galleried interior with intact seating: the dominant air of simplicity, with plain painted wooden and plaster surfaces, contrasts sharply with the sumptuously carved alabaster screen and pulpit, inserted in 1896 (Fig 35).

The government of the town was at first the responsibility of the chapel wardens and overseers of the poor, and local magistrates met fortnightly to dispense justice. By the early 19th century proper accommodation for administration was required, and a Town Hall was built over the Market Hall before 1840 (*see* Fig 37). It was described as a 'handsome, substantial brick building, in which the public business is transacted, the magistrates' meetings held, etc'[12] and it dominated the main crossroads in the town. Its loss in 1973, when it fell down, deprived Stourport of one of its most important buildings.

It was, however, commerce rather than institutions which shaped Stourport's development, and the most significant additions to the town were those which promoted business. The bridge over the Severn opened in 1775, replacing the old ferry service and making the town's commercial facilities accessible to the area on the right bank of the river. The first bridge was swept away in the great flood of 1794 and was not replaced until 1806 (Fig 36), but despite this hiatus Stourport became a market place of importance, exploiting its position at the junction of agricultural and industrial areas. Wednesday and Saturday markets existed from 1782, and agricultural produce – corn, fruit, hops, butter, eggs and poultry – were sent on to the midland industrial towns. The hop market was held on canal company land near to the Tontine Hotel, but the other produce markets were eventually located in a purpose-built market hall at the town's main crossroads (Fig 37). There were also fairs for the sale of cattle, horses and pigs. Financial facilities were somewhat

Figure 35 *The Wesleyan Methodist Chapel, Parkes Passage: the interior retains its simple seating and gallery, a stark contrast to the sumptuously carved alabaster screen, with biblical scenes and a cameo portrait of John Wesley. [DP022142, DP022141, DP022637, DP022639,]*

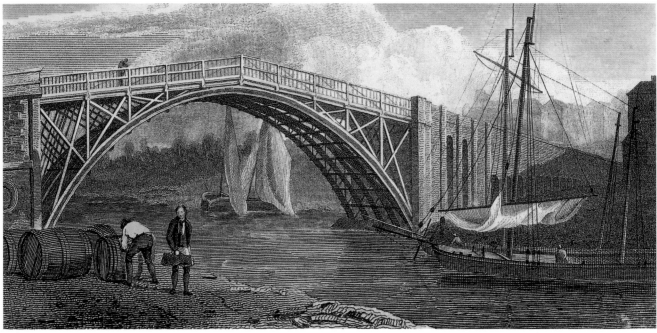

Figure 36 *(left) Stourport's bridges: the original bridge was swept away in a flood and replaced by an iron bridge in 1806. The present bridge dates from c1870. [Stourport-on-Severn Civic Society].*

Figure 37 *(right) The Market Hall, at the main crossroads in the town, was built in 1833, and later had an upper storey added to form a Town Hall. [Stourport-on-Severn Civic Society; DP022134]*

undeveloped in the early years of the town's commercial life: as late as 1841 there was no business (as opposed to savings) bank to assist the promotion of commerce, but there was a Post Office, in New Street, from at least as early as the 1820s. Among the professional services offered at the same time were those of a printer, an attorney (High Street), and a number of agents for insurance companies (two in York Street, two in Lower Mitton, and one each in New Street, High Street and Lichfield Street). All these people probably worked from offices in their houses, for in this period there was little segregation of work and domestic life.

Figure 38 *Shopfronts in the High Street: although not original, they are elegant in design. [DP022181, DP022118]*

Day-to-day provisioning requirements and more occasional specialist needs were catered for in a wide range of shops. In 1815, it was said that Stourport's streets were 'comfortable, full of shops, and thronged with people; whilst an air even of elegance pervades it'.[13] It is likely that this applied from the first decades of the town's existence. In 1828 the town could offer five bakers, four butchers, three ironmongers, two chemists, a perfumer, two hat makers, three drapers, six grocers and tea dealers, four milliners and dressmakers, eight boot and shoe makers and two china, glass and earthenware dealers. High Street was always intended as the main shopping street, but it is difficult to trace the process by which it achieved this status. Even as late as 1838, however, it was only partly commercial. Sixty-five properties are listed on the High Street in the Rate Book for that year: most were simply houses, but there were also offices, slaughterhouses, two shops, nine shops combined with live-in accommodation, and other shops combined with warehouses and, in one instance, a candlehouse.[14] The town retains some excellent shop fronts: perhaps none is original, but a number date from the 19th century and have large display windows with elegant wooden and iron fittings (Fig 38).

As a market centre, Stourport attracted large numbers of visitors, both traders and purchasers, some perhaps from a considerable distance and therefore requiring at least refreshment and perhaps accommodation as well. Where Lower Mitton probably had just two or three hostelries before the arrival of the canal (including the Red Lion, beside the main road at the Stour river crossing, and the Stourmouth Inn, now the Angel), by the late 1820s Stourport, including the village, had fourteen establishments. Social life revolved around the hotels. The largest, of course, was the Tontine, but the Swan Inn, prominently sited at the entrance to the new town at the head of the High Street, rivalled it in terms of accommodation and of its impact on the landscape (Fig 39). Both these inns had assembly rooms, that at the Swan said in 1841 to be 'often the scene of hilarity and joyous festivity'.[15] Other hotels – the White Lion and the Bell in Lion Hill – were also sizeable establishments, and some made an important contribution to the town's impression on the visitor. For example the Bridge Inn and the Crown Inn, at the northern

end of the Severn river bridge and causeway, form almost a ceremonial gateway to the town from the south (Fig 40). Other roadside or canalside pubs were humbler in their architecture: the Black Star (Fig 41) was built as a storehouse for the canal company, but was converted to a pub in the late 18th century, offering basic food and accommodation and stabling.

Although dominated by the commercial activities of the canal basin, Stourport also became an industrial centre of some importance. Both of the regionally significant industries – carpet making and iron founding – were located in the town from an early date. There was a foundry at

Figure 39 *The Swan Inn dominated the approach to the new town from the east, lying at a junction of old and new roads. It retains, in much altered form, its assembly room at the rear. [DP022075]*

Figure 40 *The approach to the town from the river bridge is framed by two inns. [DP022085]*

Figure 41 *The Black Star Inn, a canalside pub enlarged in 1884. [DP022638]*

Stourport from 1789, and the Baldwin family, the largest iron founders in the town, became renowned for their household ironmongery and kitchen ranges. Industry related to the river and canal transport was drawn to the town, sailcloth manufacturing and boat building being undertaken from the early 19th century. Other industries established in the early 19th century or earlier included vinegar making and tanning. Very little survives of this period of industrial enterprise, for many of the principal works have been entirely swept away. The built evidence for Stourport's early economic activity remains only in the canal basins and their associated buildings: the foundation of the town's wealth and reason for its existence, these have largely outlived the factories drawn to Stourport by the facilities which the town offered.

Stourport emerges into clear view in the documentary record only in the last stages of its period of greatest prosperity, when maps, trade directories, census returns and other sources fill out what we know from surviving buildings to give a good rounded picture of life in the early and mid-19th century. The urban achievement by this date had been considerable. Where fields and sandy heaths had existed in the mid-18th century there was now a substantial, if faltering, town providing its inhabitants with a wide range of urban functions. The streets were paved, a gas works provided a 'cheap and brilliant light for the streets, shops, houses, etc',[16] and the urban infrastructure, although incomplete, was new and in the main handsome and stylish. Spiritual and cultural life was catered for in a range of places of worship and educational establishments: for example, there was a subscription library in Bridge Street in 1835. Stourport had done much to justify the optimism of its now shadowy founders, but few in the early 19th century were aware that its period of greatest importance was drawing to a close.

CHAPTER 5

Stourport after 1840: diversification and adaptation

The decline in the fortunes of the Staffordshire and Worcestershire Canal Company after 1820 slowed Stourport's growth dramatically: the population rose from 2544 in 1821 to only 3012 in 1841, and actually fell in the two following decades. There was little expansion of the built-up area for half a century after 1840. On the west side of town, this was because two large villas occupied most of the available land. Moor Hall, built by Jonathan Worthington (one of the largest canal carriers) in the early 19th century and extended by the carpet manufacturer John Brinton, lay in extensive grounds, and adjacent was The Heath, built by the Heath family, also canal carriers. Only the lodges, perimeter walls and glasshouses of these mansions survive (Fig 43). In the mid and late 19th century, there was some intensification of building in the town centre, and housing for workers was provided around Baldwin's Foundry.

Figure 43 *The lodge to Moor Hall on Bewdley Road. [DP022178]*

Figure 42 *The canalside warehouse of Baldwin's foundry [DP022062]*

Newtown, a residential suburb made up mainly of modest terraced houses, was developed late in the century, after the arrival of the railway in 1862 (Fig 44).

Stourport was sustained in difficult times by its established industries. Carpet production, tanning and engineering businesses, which before 1840 were probably already more important as employers than the canal company, formed the core of local economy well into the 20th century (Fig 45, *see also* Fig 42). Baldwin's foundry, the tannery on Lombard Street, carpet factories and engineering works came to dominate parts of the town and its skyline: the tannery's huge chimney, for example, was once visible for miles around. Today, however, it is impossible to appreciate the impact of these industries on the urban landscape. Only the Vinegar Works, on the bank of the River Stour, remains as a substantial establishment, albeit with buildings mainly of the late 19th and early 20th centuries, now turned to different industrial uses.

One important aspect of the town's infrastructure was thoroughly overhauled in the second half of the 19th century. For centuries, Lower Mitton had been a chapelry within the parish of Kidderminster, but by 1844 this anachronism was recognised and it was formed into a separate ecclesiastical parish in recognition of Stourport's status as a populous town. The brick church of St Michael, built in 1790, continued to serve the parish but was seen as increasingly inadequate for contemporary needs and began to attract unfavourable comment on the grounds of its style. What, to modern eyes, seems pleasingly restrained and dignified was to the muscular evangelical Gothic enthusiasts of the 19th century 'supremely ugly' and 'very characteristic of the entire deadness to the sense of beauty which prevailed in the 18th century'[17]. Something more in the spirit of the age was required, and Sir George Gilbert Scott, the leading exponent of the Gothic revival, provided designs for a new and lavish church (Fig 46).

Constructed from 1887 after Scott's death, the new St Michael's replaced the earlier church, which was demolished and survives in plan form in the churchyard. Scott's church was never completed to the original plan, for as late as 1913 it was noted that 'the chancel and west tower included in the designs have not yet been built'.[18] It lasted only as

Figure 44 *Newtown, a suburb in the north of the town built after the arrival of the railway.* [DP022099]

Figure 45 *Nineteenth-century manufacturing industry is represented in Stourport today by the remains of the tin-stamping works on Mitton Street (left); the vinegar works beside the River Stour (right); and the canalside warehouse of Baldwin's foundry (see Fig 42). [DP022067, DP005188]*

long as its predecessor, being made into a roofless shell in the 1970s.
A new and much smaller church, opened in 1980, now occupies part of
the space, enclosed within the ruinous walls of Scott's building (Fig 47).
The whole secluded grouping – the plan of the 1782 church, Scott's
ornate building now in leafy clothing, the new church set within a quiet
garden, and a marvellous graveyard, containing monuments to many of
the principal figures in Stourport's history – is a little known treasure
(Fig 48).

The Anglican church may have had the most prominent buildings,
but it suffered from its peripheral location. The Anglican chapel at Lower
Mitton had been poorly positioned to serve the new town, and Scott's
church was similarly remote and marginal, even though the town had
expanded by the late 19th century. No such legacy hindered the
nonconformist denominations, which were the real driving force in the
town's development. They consolidated their dominance of the town
centre in the middle decades of the 19th century, building two new
chapels. The Primitive Methodist Chapel in Lickhill Lane was built in
1855 (Fig 49), smaller and humbler than its earlier Wesleyan cousin
(see Fig 35). A Congregational Chapel, with attached school room, was
built in Mitton Street in 1871. As the town expanded to the north, a new
Baptist Chapel was built on Minster Road in 1883. The three chapels
might be understated as landmarks within the town, but they represent a
strong vein of nonconformity in the local population.

Church and chapel speak for the serious and spiritual, but there was
another aspect to Stourport's life, one which focused on entertainment
and fun. This was important from the earliest days of the town. As early
as 1775 it was noted that 'this place is become the resort of people of
fashion. The beauty of the Country about it, the fine navigable Canal now
completely finished, the spacious basin for the Vessels, the River Severn
and the New Bridge over it, form altogether a very pleasing scene …
Scarcely a day passes but several Parties of Ladies and Gentlemen come
here in their Carriages'.[19] River boats brought tourists from Worcester
and further afield to marvel at the scene of commercial enterprise and
technological ingenuity. Others, however, came simply to enjoy
themselves. The presence of assembly rooms made the town a social

Figure 46 *(above) Sir George Gilbert Scott's 1876 designs for the new St Michael's Church. [Building News, 31 (1876), 312; DP006453]*

Figure 47 *(right, above) The modern church of 1980 nestles within the shell of Scott's over-ambitious building. [DP005203]*

Figure 48 *(right) Monuments in the burial ground at St Michael's Church: many of the town's most prominent citizens are buried here. [DP005206]*

Figure 49 *(far right) The humble former Primitive Methodist Chapel of 1855 on Lickhill Lane. [DP022112]*

Figure 50 *Shipley's Fairground, a permanent installation on former canal company land. [DP005199]*

Figure 51 *The park beside the river, laid out in the 20th century with a riverside promenade, putting green and bandstand and now with modern playground equipment. [DP022082]*

centre from an early period, and it never lost its attraction as a place of resort, despite the grimy nature of much of the canal's trade. By the late 19th century, concerted efforts were being made to capitalise on Stourport's assets. It had fresh air, water, and a special environment: all that was needed were better facilities to cater for visitors from less favoured areas. The newly formed Stourport Urban District Council laid out a promenade on the river bank in the 1890s, and electric trams, operating from 1898, opened up the town to day trippers from Kidderminster and the Black Country beyond. The need to entertain visitors, and to part them from their money, was recognised: a permanent fairground was established between the canal basins and the river (Fig 50), sure evidence that the canal was declining as a commercial concern, and river cruises were provided from the area of the bridge. For the more sedate visitors, a recreational park was laid out beside the river (Fig 51).

Figure 52 *Post-war public buildings: the Civic Centre of 1963, designed by Andrews and Hazzard of Birmingham (above), and the Library and Fire Station of c1970 (below). [DP022053, DP005850]*

The 20th century witnessed renewed growth in Stourport. The demolition of two large villas – Moor Hall and The Heath – released land for housing on the western side of the town, and expansion in this direction has been one of the principal features of development, with large areas of inter-war and post-Second World War housing. After the Second World War, the town spilled over to the right bank of the Severn with the development of the Walshes estate for council housing. The growing population was sustained by new industry. A power station was opened next to the river in 1926, using water transport for the delivery of coal, and in 1929 the Steatite Company, manufacturers of porcelain products, built a new factory on Bewdley Road.

The town's 20th-century development warranted the construction of a new Civic Centre to house the Urban District Council offices (Fig 52): built in 1963 by the architects Andrew and Hazzard, the Civic Centre became the main administrative offices for Wyre Forest District Council after the reorganisation of local government in 1974.

The last decades of the 20th century were difficult for Stourport. Traditional manufacturing industries – the tannery, Baldwin's Foundry, carpet making, vinegar production and engineering – all closed, as did the power station, and the railway ceased operation in 1970. 'Brownfield' sites have been used for new housing, mainly for people working in the larger towns of the region. Much, therefore, of the town's working heritage has recently been swept away. However, in a neat cyclical turn of events, Stourport is recognising its canal heritage as a unique asset. There have been some losses to the basins and their buildings, and commercial traffic ceased many years ago. But leisure use of the canals has developed considerably in recent decades, and the main basins are now busy with pleasure craft. Once again, the canal has created employment, given vitality to the town, and provided Stourport with a unique attraction for visitors and residents.

CHAPTER 6

Stourport today and in the future

Stourport-on-Severn is not a typical historic town, for its overall shape and appearance were formed during a short period in the late 18th century rather than over centuries of piecemeal development and change. Its layout, the robust visual qualities of the canal and basins, and the unity of its Georgian architecture combine to make Stourport immediately recognisable as a special town with a vigorous character: it has a real 'sense of place' (Fig 54). This book has shown that the urban landscape has changed considerably since the 18th century, but the town captured by James Sherriff's map of 1802 (*see* Fig 16) can still be clearly identified and 'read'. At the heart of modern Stourport, visitors can pick out the essential elements of the canal town much as the earliest townspeople would have seen them. And they can enjoy the town in its green, rural setting just as visitors at the turn of the 19th century did (Figs 53 and 55).

Today, at the beginning of the 21st century, Stourport faces radical change. New investment is required to develop the town's employment and provide a range of new services, and continuing housing needs must be met. A number of agencies will combine to direct this process of regeneration. The Government has laid out, in its Sustainable Communities Programme, its vision for how towns should plan for the future. The regional development agency, Advantage West Midlands, is providing funding for renewal through the Market Towns Programme, and the local regeneration partnership, Stourport Forward, set up in September 2004, has developed an ambitious programme to improve conditions for local companies, enhance Stourport's environment and provide opportunities for training and access to work for local people. Wyre Forest District Council is at the centre of plans for regeneration, and local people, too, are involved in decision making, as Stourport Civic Society, so instrumental in the past in devising solutions to problems, also has a voice in the debate about future directions.

Renewal and regeneration need not mean sweeping away all that remains of the past. 'Quality of life' is about jobs, services and housing conditions, but it is also about the environment, about creating places where people want to live, work and visit. A town's special character is increasingly being seen as a major asset to be exploited, and of course the historic environment is a key element in providing identity. Conservation,

Figure 53 *The Angel Inn in its riverside setting* [DP022092]

Figure 54 *Stourport from the air, taken in 2005. [NMR 24103/04 SO 8171/4]*

Figure 55 *The link between town and countryside is an important part of the character of Stourport; the busy boatyard is seen against a green backdrop of countryside to the west, with the tower of Areley Kings church in the middle distance. [DP022170]*

therefore, lies at the heart of the renewal process, accommodating and welcoming change but managing it so that historic buildings and landscapes are retained and revitalised.

Stourport's rich historic environment provides a unique resource, and today's challenge is to combine effective and imaginative presentation of the town's historic character with economic success and good and appropriate new design. The historic town remains a living, working, and changing entity and the issue is not whether change should take place, but rather determining what role the evidence of Stourport's origins, development and history should play in the process of change.

Despite some significant losses, Stourport still has a vast amount of historic built fabric, much of it protected by provisions within England's

highly developed system of legal powers. There are 102 listed buildings in the parish, including parts of the canal infrastructure,[20] and the historic centre of the town is protected by the designation of four conservation areas.[21] The responsibility for managing this system of legal measures rests with Wyre Forest District Council and, in the case of archaeology, Worcestershire County Council, both of which employ specialist staff to advise and negotiate with applicants as part of the planning process. The District Council is also carrying out a survey of 'locally listed' buildings to identify those buildings which may not meet the criteria for statutory protection but which nevertheless contribute to the district's distinctive character (Fig 56).

Legal powers have been introduced at different times since the late 19th century and have formed a rather untidy and sometimes confusing patchwork of controls. They have also tended to present a picture of historic places as collections of designated fragments which are 'controlled' rather than as seamless historic entities where change should be managed in the light of a particular set of agreed priorities. The present government is introducing changes to the way historic places are designated and managed both to make the system easier to understand and to deal with; and to recognise historic places as having stories to tell, illustrating the distinctiveness of localities and settlements which cannot be related solely through designated assets.

Successful conservation depends not just upon the designation of the principal historic assets but also on sensitivity and vision in their treatment while undergoing change. Leading the way in the promotion of the town's historic character are changes to the canal and its infrastructure, the most distinctive features of Stourport's legacy from the past. There have been many changes to this resource over the last century and more: for example, both Lichfield and Cheapside Basins have been infilled. Weathering and wear and damage in use are normal parts of the life of any structure and repair and renewal is often complex and costly (Fig 57). The canal fabric benefits by having a single owner, British Waterways, and therefore a single management regime. Given the untapped value of the basins and the significant opportunity which they could provide in stimulating the local economy, British Waterways

Figure 56 *The origin of these plaques on houses in Mart Lane is not evident. Their intention is good but their wording does not reflect either current or proposed conservation legislation. [DP004906]*

Figure 57 *An example of erosion, wear and tear and potentially damaging plant growth on stonework and brickwork of canal structures. [DP022205]*

initiated their recovery by submitting a £3.1 million conservation and regeneration bid to the Heritage Lottery Fund (HLF) in 2002. The programme, which draws in a number of partners to work with British Waterways, aims to safeguard the future of this nationally important complex through the repair of its canalside structures, landscape enhancement, archaeology, community development and habitat improvements. British Waterways was awarded £1.7 million in March 2005 towards the ambitious four-year programme. Furthermore, plans for the former Lichfield Basin site demonstrate how historic character can be restored; the scheme for new housing here includes provision for the reopening of part of the original basin and for linking it, by a new bridge on Mart Lane, to the existing main expanse of water

(Fig 58). The Tontine, which this book has identified as one of the most remarkable canal-related buildings in England, offers another opportunity for reuse, both securing the future of the building and contributing life and activity to the river frontage and the quays. Only a Public Inquiry saved it from demolition in 1977.

So the conservation of the canal and its structures looks secure for the foreseeable future. However, the buildings of the town, with a multiplicity of ownerships and a diverse range of problems, offer an entirely different challenge. There have been serious losses in recent decades: the Town Hall was demolished in 1973 following its partial collapse, and more recently the garden walls of York House were demolished as part of the residential development of the adjacent site. That development blocked the historic view from York Street across the basins and a key visual link between the town and the basins was severed.

Ostensibly minor change to historic buildings has the potential to destroy or weaken historic character. The replacement of timber sash windows, made for the property probably in a joiner's workshop nearby, by mass produced uPVC is one of the most obvious types of such change and one of the most damaging to the subtle historic pattern of Stourport's Georgian buildings. Careless replacement and painting of shopfronts, not always within the control of the planning system, has further nibbled away at Stourport's historic character (Fig 59). Erosion of smaller elements of the historic built environment such as boundary walls also adds to a picture which sometimes seems discouraging.

Figure 58 *The new bridge on Mart Lane will allow boats to use the reopened Lichfield Basin (left); Coping from the parapet of the new bridge on Mart Lane: the use of traditional brick and natural sandstone ties in a modern structure to the historical pattern of materials in the town (right). [DP022194, DP022195]*

Figure 59 *Shopfronts: historic elements remain alongside later alterations but there is plenty of scope to provide a shopfront that better complements the 18th-century building it forms part of without losing commercial pulling power (above); One of a pair of good quality, probably 19th-century, shopfronts in the High Street (below). [DP022191, DP022182]*

Property owners can, however, respond well to a demonstration of the benefits of more sensitive treatment of historic buildings, realising both the aesthetic and, in many cases, the financial advantages offered by the use of historically appropriate techniques, materials and components. The Lottery-funded works by British Waterways will provide a set of good examples which could be followed in the other buildings in the town. But observation of Stourport's historic buildings and their maintenance can provide examples of the correct use of lime mortar pointed to a correct profile, of historically informed designs of windows and doors, and of the appropriate choice and maintenance of items such as ironwork and gutters and downpipes (Fig 60). Treatment of open spaces can also benefit from the application of good conservation principles. The improvement of the garden at the Methodist Church in Parkes Passage will allow it to be enjoyed by the whole community and will complement recent repairs to the church building, grant-aided under a scheme funded by English Heritage and the Heritage Lottery Fund (Fig 61).

Attention to the sensitive care of old buildings is, of course, only one aspect of regeneration. At the other end of the scale is the redevelopment of large 'brownfield' sites, for the opportunities which these provide for dominant new buildings have the potential to radically transform the appearance of a town. Stourport has a number of such sites, for example on the eastern side of town are the former Carpets of Worth and vinegar factory sites, and land in the central area, between Bridge Street and the Clock Basin, lies right in the heart of the old town. All the brownfield sites present Stourport with a great opportunity for beneficial change and growth, but each opportunity poses questions. It will greatly benefit the town to bring in more people to support local businesses. This will in turn generate money for the maintenance and repair of the town's historic buildings. But ways will have to be found to manage the extra traffic that those people will produce in a town which already suffers from congestion and high levels of through traffic crossing the Severn. Questions also arise as to whether people visiting the basins and the shops and other attractions in the new development will be encouraged to explore the High Street and spend some of their money there. To this

Figure 60 *Historic detail: Georgian door and doorcase (left, top); bootscraper in New Street (left, bottom); Georgian sash windows and good-quality pointing in Lichfield Street (above). [DP022175, DP005201, DP022198]*

end, Wyre Forest District Council and British Waterways have explored opportunities to improve the connection from Bridge Street into the heart of the basins complex.

At the centre of the debate about the future of Stourport is the design of new development. This is a contentious subject on which there are few answers that are absolutely right or wrong. Design is more than a superficial issue. Designing new buildings, to demanding modern standards, that complement and harmonise with historic buildings but reflect the life and culture of the time in which they were built, is a challenge for the architect. When the challenge is successfully met the result can enhance the way we see and enjoy both the old and new buildings. If the historic town of Stourport is to gain the maximum benefit from the large area of new development, the design of that development will have to both emphasise the quality and individuality of historic Stourport and provide something that is clearly a contribution from the early 21st century to sit harmoniously within it. In the recent past the design of new buildings in Stourport has attempted, not always successfully, to copy the Georgian architecture of the town, but there should always be scope for introducing new ideas and materials: the issue is not whether a new building conforms to a common style, but whether, in its form, scale and contribution to the urban landscape, it is appropriate to a historic setting (Fig 62).

Successful conservation-based regeneration depends upon understanding and appreciation of historic places and of the significance of elements within them. That understanding should shape the thinking behind redevelopment and reflect the values placed on the historic environment by a wide range of stakeholders. It is necessary for both paid and voluntary conservation specialists but is also important for enjoyment by the public at large. Stourport shows that both the building and the use of structured understanding of the historic environment are matters for local people as well as professional specialists. Since 1968 the town has benefited from the work of an active Civic Society, which has played a significant role in planning issues, campaigning for the conservation of Stourport's unique historic environment as well as taking the initiative in direct actions like the restoration of the Baldwin

Figure 61 *A modern landscape design provides a fresh new setting for the 18th-century Methodist Church.* *[DP022171]*

Figure 62 *Recent housing development on Parkes Quay uses the setting of the canal to make a pleasant residential environment. The approach to design represents only one way to incorporate new development into a historic setting (above); New housing on Parkes Passage uses traditional details and materials to respond to its historic setting (right).* [DP004905, DP022057]

monuments in St Michael's Churchyard (*see* Fig 48). Local people are also active in a project, called 'Unlocking Stourport's Past', to record and photograph small and often overlooked items like historic paving, bollards and nameplates (Fig 63). The lottery-funded programme for the canal basins is also encouraging local people to understand and enjoy their historic environment through a programme of education, interpretation and artists' commissions, including the opportunity for events like temporary lighting displays around the site (Fig 64).

Public understanding of historic places enhances enjoyment of them and builds support for their proper conservation and the careful management of change within them. This is the key to the long-term care of England's historic places. More than that, the regeneration of historic towns like Stourport is underpinned by popular interest in them and enjoyment of their distinctive qualities. Specialists in the study and management of historic places help to provide a framework for understanding. But the example of Stourport-on-Severn shows that committed local groups, residents, businesses and visitors all have important parts to play in the proper care of the historic town and the management of change for its future.

Figure 63 *(above) Cast-iron bollard in Raven Street: an example of the incidental historic details of the town recorded by the Unlocking Stourport's Past project. [DP022189]*

Figure 64 *(left) Art agency pro/POSIT tests projections on the Iron Warehouse in September 2004 to develop ideas for future art events. [British Waterways and pro/POSIT 2004]*

Notes

1 Nash 1799, 47

2 Defoe 1724–6 (Penguin edn 1971), 370

3 Staffordshire Record Office (SRO) Minute book of proprietors of SWC, 19 Sept 1769

4 British Waterways Archives (BWA) SWC collection, Leases 70/91, 5 Dec 1799

5 SRO, Minute book of proprietors of SWC, 1771

6 BWA SWC collection, Leases 70/88, 25 Aug 1808

7 Nicholson 1813, 137–8

8 *Berrow's Worcester Journal*, 14 Sept 1775

9 Worcestershire Record Office (WRO), Deeds and leases 705:550, BA4600/890ii; 705:550, BA4600/23

10 Burton 1890, 137–8

11 WRO, Deeds and leases 705:550, BA5351/4

12 Bentley 1841, 114

13 Laird 1815, 248

14 WRO, 1838 Rate Book, 899:310,BA10470/221

15 Bentley 1841, 111

16 Bentley 1841, 113

17 Burton 1890, 126

18 VCH Worcester 3, 175

19 Trinder 1987, 60

20 All listed buildings are regarded as of national interest and they are listed against national criteria. Buildings are listed in one of three grades indicating their level of architectural or historic character. Of Stourport's listed buildings none are in grade I, 4 are in grade II★(star), and 98 in grade II. Apart from the absence of grade I buildings this reflects the proportions of buildings in those grades nationally.

21 A conservation area is *an area of special architectural or historic interest the character or appearance of which it is desirable to preserve or enhance*. Conservation areas are designated by the local authority and introduce legal powers over demolition and some other changes together with an opportunity for the local authority to manage change within the area through the planning system in a way that ensures that it preserves or enhances the area. The conservation areas in Stourport are: (i) Stourport number 1 including the canal basins, riverside, and adjoining streets; (ii) Stourport number 2 which includes the central part of the Georgian town; (iii) Gilgal which covers Lower Mitton; and (iv) part of the Staffordshire and Worcestershire Canal Conservation Area.

References and further reading

Bentley 1841 *Bentley's History, Guide and Directory of the borough of Kidderminster and Bewdley*. Birmingham

Bradford, A 2002 *Stourport-on-Severn: a history of the town and the area*. Redditch: Hunt End Books

Burton, J R 1890 *A History of Kidderminster*. Elliott Stock: London

Carter, A 2000 *Stourport-on-Severn: Images of England*. Stroud: Stourport-on-Severn Civic Society and Tempus Publishing

Cross-Rudkin, P 2005 'Constructing the Staffordshire and Worcestershire Canal, 1766--72'. *Transactions of the Newcomen Society*, **75**, 289–304

Crowe, N 1994 *The English Heritage Book of Canals*. London: Batsford

Defoe, D 1724–6 *A Tour Through the Whole Island of Great Britain* (Rogers, P (ed) Penguin edn 1971. Harmondsworth: Penguin)

Godfrey Edition 2002 'Stourport 1901' Old Ordnance Survey Maps, Worcestershire Sheet 14.10. Consett: Alan Godfrey

Laird, F C A 1815 *A Topographical and Historical Description of the County of Worcester*. Sherwood, Neely and Jones: London

Nash, Dr T R 1799 *Supplement to the Collections for the History of Worcestershire*. London

Nicholson, G 1813 *The Cambrian Traveller's Guide*, 2nd ed. Stourport

Pigot, J and Co 1828 *National Commercial Directory, Worcestershire*, 878–9. London

Porteous, J D 1977 Canal Ports: *The Urban Achievement of the Canal Age*. London: Academic Press

Randell, J 1882 *The Severn Valley: a series of sketches, descriptive and pictorial, of the course of the Severn*, etc. Madeley

Trinder, B 1987 *The Making of the Industrial Landscape* Sutton: Gloucester

The Victoria History of the County of Worcester Vol 2 1906; Vol 3 1913; and Vol 4 1924. London

Other titles in the series

Behind the Veneer: The South Shoreditch furniture trade and its buildings.
Joanna Smith and Ray Rogers, 2006.
Product code 51204, ISBN 9781873592960

The Birmingham Jewellery Quarter: An introduction and guide.
John Cattell and Bob Hawkins, 2000.
Product code 50204, ISBN 9781850747772

Built to Last? The buildings of the Northamptonshire boot and shoe industry.
Kathryn A Morrison with Ann Bond, 2004.
Product code 50921, ISBN 9781873592793

Gateshead: Architecture in a changing English urban landscape.
Simon Taylor and David Lovie, 2004.
Product code 52000, ISBN 9781873592762

Manchester: The Northern Quarter.
Simon Taylor and Julian Holder, 2007.
Product code 50946, ISBN 9781873592847

Manchester: The warehouse legacy – An introduction and guide.
Simon Taylor, Malcolm Cooper and P S Barnwell, 2002.
Product code 50668, ISBN 9781873592670

Newcastle's Grainger Town: An urban renaissance.
Fiona Cullen and David Lovie, 2003.
Product code 50811, ISBN 9781873592779

'One Great Workshop': The buildings of the Sheffield metal trades.
Nicola Wray, Bob Hawkins and Colum Giles, 2001.
Product code 50214, ISBN 9781873592663

Storehouses of Empire: Liverpool's historic warehouses.
Colum Giles and Bob Hawkins, 2004.
Product code 50920, ISBN 9781873592809

£7.99 each (plus postage and packing)

To order
Tel: EH Sales 01761 452966
Email: ehsales@gillards.com

Online bookshop: www.english-heritage.org.uk

Central Stourport today, showing the location of the main buildings mentioned in the text

KEY

1	Canal basins	24	Baptist Chapel
2	Tontine Hotel	25	St Michael and All Angels Church
3	Iron Warehouse and canal office	26	Church of St Michael (demolished)
4	Clock Warehouse	27	Red Lion Inn
5	York House	28	Tin plate works
6	Warehouse	29	Canal water feeder pump (site of)
7	Mart Lane houses and warehouse	30	Carpet factory (site of)
8	Angel Inn	31	Power station (site of)
9	Shipley's fairground	32	Vinegar works
10	Engine house	33	Riverside park
11	River bridge and causeway	34	Civic Centre
12	Crown and Bridge Inns	35	The Heath (site of)
13	Town Hall and Market Hall (site of)	36	Moor Hall (site of)
14	Wesleyan Chapel	37	Lodge to Moor Hall
15	Canal maintenance yard		
16	Swan Inn		
17	Primitive Methodist Chapel		
18	Black Star Inn		
19	Congregational Chapel		
20	Tannery (site of)		
21	Baldwin's foundry (site of) and canalside warehouse		
22	Foundry (site of)		
23	Library, Police Station, Fire station		

Back cover
The Severn Bridge Trust's heraldic arms, a detail in cast iron on the Severn river bridge of 1870. [DP005193]